Andrew Barber

Cowboys

*Illustrated by Gian Paolo Faleschini
and Edoardo Marinelli*

OXFORD
UNIVERSITY PRESS

This book belongs to

OXFORD
UNIVERSITY PRESS

Great Clarendon Street, Oxford OX2 6DP

Oxford University Press is a department of the University of Oxford.
It furthers the University's objective of excellence in research, scholarship,
and education by publishing worldwide in

Oxford New York

Auckland Bangkok Buenos Aires Cape Town Chennai
Dar es Salaam Delhi Hong Kong Istanbul Karachi Kolkata
Kuala Lumpur Madrid Melbourne Mexico City Mumbai
Nairobi São Paulo Shanghai Singapore Taipei Tokyo Toronto

with an associated company in Berlin

Oxford is a registered trade mark of Oxford University Press
in the UK and in certain other countries

Text copyright © Andrew Barber 2002
Illustrations copyright © Gian Paulo Faleschini and Edoardo Marinelli 2002

The moral rights of the author and artist have been asserted

First published 2002

Paperback ISBN 0-19-910635-5

1 3 5 7 9 10 8 6 4 2

Printed in Spain by Edelvives.

Contents

▶ What do you know about cowboys?

Cowboys are often in films or on the TV but these are actors. The best way to find out about **real** cowboys is to go back in time…

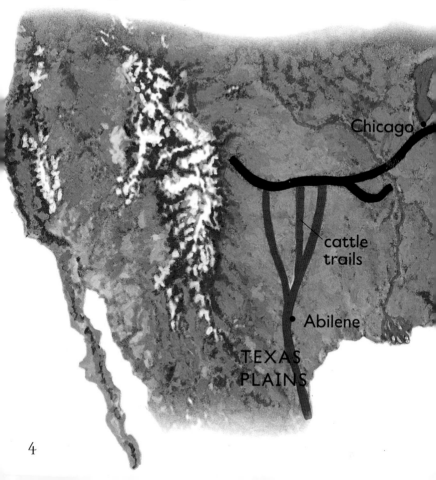

Chicago

cattle trails

• Abilene

TEXAS PLAINS

Imagine that you are in Texas,
in North America, 120 years ago.

Imagine wide, grassy plains,
stretching as far as you can see.

Imagine half-wild cattle with long,
curved horns, grazing on the grass.

These Texas cattle are
being fattened up for
market. They will feed
hungry city folks in
places like Chicago
and New York.

railway
lines

New
York

Now imagine a dust cloud on the horizon. It's coming closer… and closer. Two tough, weather-beaten men, thin as string beans, are riding across the range.

They are cowboys: Pete and his buddy Flood. They are out rounding up cattle.

A cowboy's equipment

a **bedroll** is just one or two rough blankets

the wide brim of a **stetson** keeps off the sun and rain

bandanna is a scarf to keep off dust and sweat

the **Western saddle** is comfortable on long rides

gloves stop rope-burn

the **lariat** is a long rope with a loop in it, for catching cattle

chaps are tough leather leggings to keep out thorns

Western boots have deep heels that don't get stuck in the stirrups

spurs

▶ The round-up

Pete and Flood work for the Bar E ranch. The Bar E is a huge cattle farm. It has over 5000 longhorns. All the cattle are marked with a brand, so that people know they belong to the Bar E.

ranch house

bunk house

Spring is round-up time. The cowboys gather together all the cattle, and brand the new calves.

The Bar E
The ranch house is where the cattle owner lives. Nearby is a bunk house where the cowboys sleep, and a cook house where they eat.

corrals

stables

cook house

Pete and Flood have rounded up lots of cattle. Flood takes them back to the ranch, while Pete stays to look for strays. He sees one in a narrow valley, and charges down the slope after it.

Yee-hah! How does he stay on that horse?

The stray tries to get away, but Pete and his horse head it off.

Did you know...
Hundreds of years before cattle came to Texas, there were cowboys in Mexico. They were called **vaqueros** ('vac-air-ohs'). Like Texas cowboys, they carried lariats and wore chaps.

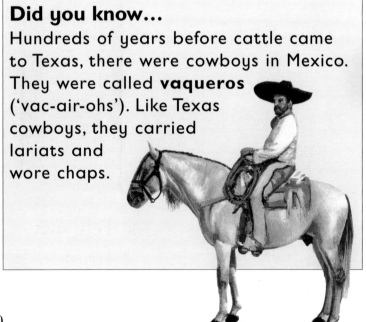

After a few hours' work, Pete has
caught quite a bunch of strays.
He drives them back to the ranch.

Branding the calves

The Bar E cowboys have gathered together a huge herd of cattle. Now this year's calves have to be separated from the other cattle for branding.

Catching young calves in the packed herd is tricky work. But Pete's horse is smart. She can follow a calf's every twist and turn.

Once a calf is separated from the herd, Pete twirls his lariat and throws. The loop catches the calf's back heels, and it crashes to the ground.

Before the calf can
get up, another
cowboy runs up
and holds its head.

Now a third cowboy
arrives with a smoking-hot
branding iron.

SSSSS

There is a hiss, and a smell of
burning. The calf bellows with pain,
but it is over in an instant. The Bar
E brand is burnt on the calf's skin.

SSSSSSSS!

Once the calves have been branded, they are let loose until next year. But the older cattle have to go to market to be sold.

the bar E brand

▶ On the trail

The cattle market is at Abilene,
hundreds of miles to the north.
The cattle have to walk all the way.

Pete and fourteen other cowboys
will look after the cattle on the trail.

Flood is the trail boss.
'Move 'em out!' he calls.

The chuck wagon

Behind the herd comes the cook, rattling along in the chuck wagon. It carries food and supplies for the trip.

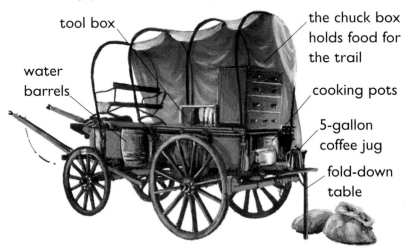

tool box

the chuck box holds food for the trail

water barrels

cooking pots

5-gallon coffee jug

fold-down table

The herd has been travelling for two days now. The cattle move slowly, eating as they go.

A river runs across the trail here. There are no bridges. How will the herd get across?

"YEEEEE-HAH!"

Pete and the other cowboys yell and wave their hats. They chase the leaders of the herd into the water.

Did you know...
Cowboys from Argentina in South America were called **gauchos** ('gow-chos'). They didn't use a lariat: they threw a bolas. A bolas has three heavy balls joined with rope, and it tangles round the cattle's legs.

Once in the water, the cattle head for the other bank. Pete rides his horse alongside the leaders, to make sure they don't turn back.

▶ Campfire

It's the end of a long, hot, dusty day. Time to stop for the night.

The cowboys sit round the camp fire, eating and talking. One cowboy plays a fiddle. Others start a card game.

Pete and another cowboy have to watch the herd for the first part of the night. They ride around the cattle to keep them together.

Pete sings along with the fiddler. The cattle seem to like it!

▶ Storm!

Late in the night, there is a flash of lightning. BABOOOM! – a terrible storm breaks. The steers take fright, and charge away into the dark.

In a moment, every cowboy is on his
horse and galloping after the herd.
They must stop them! Pete and two
others catch up with the herd leaders.
They force their horses against the
steers, to make them turn.

It's working!

The cattle keep running, but in a
circle. Eventually, they calm down.

▶ Trail's end

Pete and the others are on the trail for six weeks. There are more storms, rivers, and a burning hot desert to cross.

Then, one day, they see buildings in the distance.

Yeeee - hah!

It's the end of the trail.

The cattle are sold.
They go on trains to the cities.

The cowboys get paid. They spend
all their money on fine new clothes,
on drinking and on gambling!

After the trail drive, it's back to the ranch. There's plenty to do over the summer, and in autumn there's a smaller round-up.

Did you know...
Hawaii is a group of islands in the Pacific Ocean. Even here, there were cowboys, called **paniolas**. Paniolas decorated their hats with a band of flowers and feathers.

But winter is a bad time for the
cowboys. There is not enough work
on the ranch. Some cowboys find
work nearby. Some stay on the
ranch and ride wolf patrol, keeping
wolf packs away from the herd.

But Pete has a different job
over the winter.

He's a rodeo rider in Buffalo
Bill's Wild West Show.

Ride 'em cowboy!

Did you know...
There are still cowboys today, although
they often ride in trucks instead of on
horses. The best place to see cowboy
skills today is at a rodeo. You can
watch cattle roping,
bronco riding,
bareback riding,
bull riding and steer
wrestling!

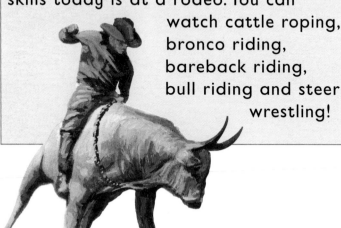

Glossary

This glossary will help you to understand what some important words mean. You can find them in this book by using the page numbers given below.

brand A brand is a mark on a cow to show who it belongs to.   **9, 14**

brand When cowboys brand cattle they burn the mark on the cow's skin.   **8, 12, 15**

corral A corral is a fenced area on a ranch where cowboys can brand calves, or train new horses.   **9**

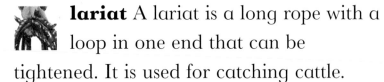

lariat A lariat is a long rope with a loop in one end that can be tightened. It is used for catching cattle.   **7, 10, 13, 18**

longhorn Longhorns are a kind of Texas cattle.   **8**

ranch A ranch is a very big cattle farm. **8, 9, 26, 27**

 range The plains of Texas were called the range. **6**

 rodeo A rodeo is a competition to test cowboy skills, such as riding, roping and branding. **28**

 round-up A round-up is what happens when cowboys gather all a ranch's cattle together. They can then check that none are hurt or lost, and brand any new calves. **9, 26**

 spurs Spurs are sharp spikes that cowboys wear on their boots. Spurs make the horse go faster. **7**

 stray A stray is a cow or calf that has got separated from the main herd. **10, 11**

Reading Together

Oxford Reds have been written by leading children's authors who have a passion for particular non-fiction subjects. So as well as up-to-date information, fascinating facts and stunning pictures, these books provide powerful writing which draws the reader into the text.

Oxford Reds are written in simple language, checked by educational advisors. There is plenty of repetition of words and phrases, and all technical words are explained. They are an ideal vehicle for helping your child develop a love of reading – by building fluency, confidence and enjoyment.

You can help your child by reading the first few pages out loud, then encourage him or her to continue alone. You could share the reading by taking turns to read a page or two. Or you could read the whole book aloud, so your child knows it well before tackling it alone.

Oxford Reds will help your child develop a love of reading and a lasting curiosity about the world we live in.

Sue Palmer
Writer and Literacy Consultant